THE CLEARING

POEMS

LISA HITON

THE CLEARING

POEMS

LISA HITON

BLACK LAWRENCE PRESS

Black
Lawrence
Press

www.blacklawrence.com

Executive Editor: Diane Goettel
Chapbook Editor: Lisa Fay Coutley
Cover and Book Design: Zoe Norvell

"Dream of My Father's Shiva, Lake Michigan, 1963," "Sky in Excess"
(appears as "Moon Child" here), "Mahler's Ninth," "In Response to Trees," "Dream of
My Father's Shiva, Auschwitz, 1942," and "Horseshoe" originally appeared in Lisa Hiton's
full length collection, *Afterfeast*, Tupelo Press, 2020. Used by permission of the publisher.

Published 2022 by Black Lawrence Press.
Printed in the United States.

Table of Contents

I.

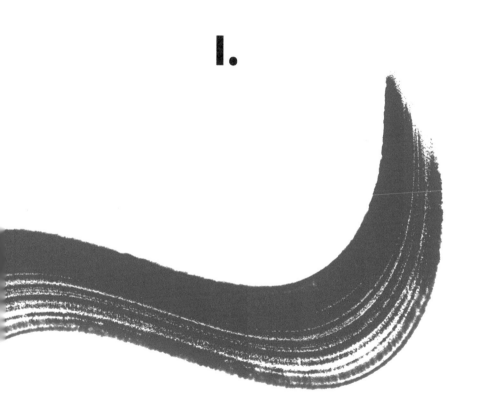

Dream of My Father's Shiva, Lake Michigan, 1963

I pull a body out of the lake and it's my size.
You are completely dry.
I drag you across the beach by the right arm
and right leg. I bring you to the shiva house.
It's easy because you grip my hand.
I don't have to do all the work.
Your other hand is missing fingers.
I trawl you back to the lake to find them.
Your freckles enumerate
and cluster, constellations, little myths
I flick off your skin like sand.
The sand dissolves into snow, which turns
to ice. I slide with you,
ice skating children playing on a snow day.
Faces of the family around the shiva table
seasons later, years later, waiting for us
to return from this desert of ice.
The hours, they come as an urn
to put you in. You do not fit
anywhere else—the mind, the house, the vase…
I am not prepared for the change:
when the grip tightens and then slacks,
it's winter, it's summer.

Shiksa

Father drops the Swarovski ornament.
The dog comes running like it might be meat.

I watch through the window in the backyard

when she starts crying
over a Christmas tree. *My father*

gave me that one. They clean the crystal
and go upstairs.

I walk back to my house

thinking about my mother
and father tucking me into bed.

She would read me a story and leave

so my father and I could sing *sh'ma*. Now I've grown
into my Jewess curls. Each summer, the sun dyes

less and less blond streaks into my hair.

I thought about hanging a mezuzah in my apartment doorway
and imagined men running in the other direction

repulsed by my mother's lips

and his Ashkenazi cheeks. I bite the urge to say
shiksa when she invites me to stop over for brunch.

I think of my mother

her coarse brown hair, her Spanish skin. She tells me
Take the high road. You are the adult.

I swallow the word with soufflé
across the table from her burly sons

their faces shining in the twinkle lights.

Till

A windmill tenses its rubberband hold and
releases a wind. Wind in tides, a voice, rippling the lake
of grass. A sea of vitriols below, bone-still, breath held.

Pricks of light, fog lifting, a barbed fence wound round
the grey slate building where a plow homes. Upwind
chatter coaxes, flowers nuzzle the plow's foot. Rusted

gear unwinds at nightfall, screeches, whirs its foot out
of the mud. Raking hand cuts a wound on earth. An
urnful of eyelashes, binoculars, bar soap. Fate, never

small as a keyhole. The keyhole, a furrow, when the seeds
don't feed, swallows a plow, an urn, the bones, blooms
obliteration by daffodil growth. And somewhere a windmill

cuts, unravels its winds: a shiver for every grass blade's
spine, cooling of crud and rust, its path winding, its
shrilling secret, an acerbic lacuna, begging to unearth.

Moon Child

I think of these things to tell you when you are asleep:
Little pools of water filled with limbs. The sky is dull,
The sky in excess. I draw rings around your belly.

Sometimes I do things to you because I want you to do them to me.

In the morning, when you are still asleep, I reach my hand
Into your mouth, down through your chest. I turn your heart over.

Beyond the Grasses in the Clearing

You'll arrive at the woods. Beyond the woods, there will be a river. Follow the river until daylight breaks again. There will be a large wooden box painted blue. Even though the box is wooden, you will not be able to break it with an axe. Look for the hunter's skull. What's left of the jaw will do the trick. If you can get inside, past the wood and ice and black space, there will be an animal. If the animal is an animal, you have failed. If the animal is not an animal, but a woman, gently take off her shoes. If her feet are warm, she is alive. If she is alive, she is going to die.

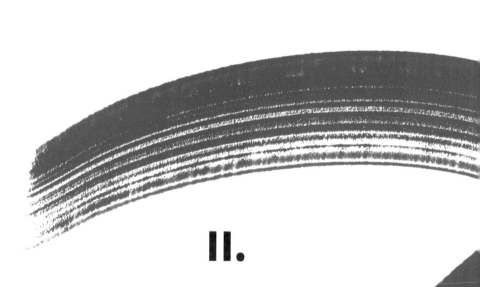

II.

Dream of My Father's Shiva, McCoy Park, 1976

Under the twelve inches of fresh powder, I smell the loam of the
place—
I want to make little pots for you, my thumb in the thick of it,
fingers pinching.

They were supposed to be little pots, but now it's just one jug, and
the jug is an urn.
The urn is full of you: there's a gravestone in Chicago with your
name on it

but you would not get in the coffin. I am in Colorado where we
never lived.
I don't want to burn you to ashes, but I'm already carrying the jug.

Don't make me do this. There's a dining room full of Jews sitting
shiva
a thousand miles north of this godforsaken mountain. It's summer
there

and it does not smell like clay. (In my life there's a brother—
why won't he materialize?—) I snowshoe up the mountain, dust
of you

spilling over the sides. I won't throw it to the wind, or the pink
chimney smoke,
or the haze of barking dogs lapping up lake water, waiting.

No Sea

Camels on the horizon, silhouettes of children riding them
        out past the waterfalls of Setti Fatma. When I can't sleep
this is what I count. Swift, windblown,

    until there are so many paths that they gallop in zigzags
        like the motorbikes through souks on Marrakech nights.
    At first it's simple: one two three four five six then

sand kicking up and hanging in the impenetrable air
                then the counting: touch me touch me touch me
        sand piled, camels in many desert holes,
            scent of yellow jasmine but with no flower in sight
        it can only be you, approaching me like a tide
            from behind, wiping the sand from my eyes.

    Tell me it's simple: one two three four love you love
                you love. The heart, an image of ruined land
    going up in flames: no sea, no tide, the animal
            never kneeling, mapless lovers

            walking the tightrope night at the circus school.
    Tell me it's simple: right left right left you wrung out
            on the clothesline in the desert sun, dried

apricots, jarred on the windowsill: no
I don't want to love you anymore, no I don't want to be
waiting under a dream of sand like the princess at the bottom
of the hourglass. Say nothing. Here is the jar,

here is the shriveled heart inside the jar, here is the screw top
to lock it in. This is the message in a bottle placed in the satchel
of the camel, walking the horizon of fire: no sea no tide
never a way to reach you.

Beach Fossil Funeral

Bleached, bleached discs
pile this moment
of South Caroline shore,
a days-earlier sandbar—you

lure me, bioluminescence
ablaze in the indiscernible
dark. Conviction
posing as stars.

I place my hand in.
The black ink proffers its advice:
be taken, be taken—

discs piled at the dweller's feet. Egret,
pedestrian, stray dog. They're called
to the fossils as though they were

the treasure of Atlantis.
I watch them petrify,
abandon change for permanence—

when you die it is decided
what you will become

by what you are taken by:

the sepulchral chants of you
padding my skin like gauze.

Visitation

She appeared in the morning. She waited outside my door,
golden branch cutters in her hands. I hear voices—none of them
   hers.
Time to cut loose they say. They signal wind and forgiveness. But I
   move
from the piano, across the floor and let her in. The phantoms
call off the notes of Brahms. But I recall
her to life, there on the hardwood. Her
arms around me, a memory. The branch cutters
between us, cleaving

Portrait in a Jewelry Box

You have inherited everything.
But the earrings and the box,

those were stolen.
You had checked in

to a hotel on Queen's Gate.
They'd been left

on the nightstand. By the time
the woman who owned them

came back,
they were already stowed

in your weekend tote
(wrapped in a chambray

stolen from the last woman you adored).
At this hour, intent in the mirror,

you see yourself, but feel nothing.
It is when you look in the jewelry box,

touch your fingers to the bottom,
that fear consumes you:

you hadn't gone to my funeral;
when I was asked if

I'd like to be ghost or object
I chose this little coffin.

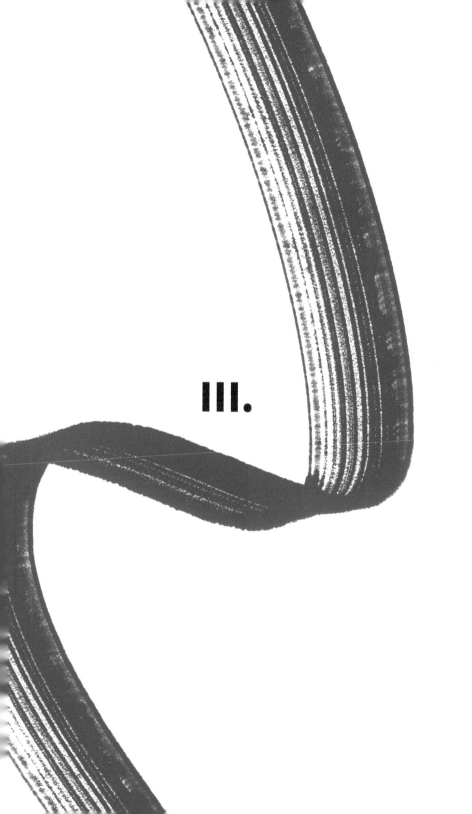

III.

Picnic

the youth take an afternoon fieldtrip to the fields
of Auschwitz   playing tag   bored by the flat flat emerald

"Wie viele?"   "Es macht nichts."

brown bag   cola bottles   whumping heels
halt at a chaperone's whistle   nitrogen-blown bags for potato
chips   the crumbs of which leave oil on denim   salt on dirt

Mahler's Ninth

Gone, the pile
of shut black
mouths bowled
in cold

water. Gone
the thyme and tang of shallot,
as the garlic
burns in the oil.

They whir when strained:
shhh, let them think
we're already

gone. Does a thing remember
its ocean? Brine
like ragged
cement. O

what thrill their lives were,
before the ice bath!
before the plastic bag!
In goes the white

wine and the fog
that rises from them
makes them drowsy—

why did I bring
something alive
into this kitchen,

in the wake of what struggle
am I to offer or perform
myself,

what was happening
in there, in those
blooming mouths—

so I peeked inside
through the steam,
obsessed with death
but having no desire to die.

Egyptian Daydream

No one seen near the arch
of reeds after exile. What
to make of the images: soap,
lampshade, locusts, blood,
the chicken schmaltz
curdled and floating in the broth.

In Response to Trees

In winter I knew them all
as one dead thing,

but now I love to watch them blossom.

The shortest tree
seems Japanese, translates

beauty into sunlike white and pink.

I lie under them
deciphering

their shapes. How to give a name
to something you know so well: Mother,

I know you are afraid

of my love
when I watch the little round discs fall

suicidally toward me. I am afraid

of what I might call them
while they are in the air...

     Mother, I want to call them,
my Katarina, my riad, my morning floor,

tiny petals like eyelids
dropping down. The first time I dreamt

of falling
it was peaceful like this:—

nameless world, filled with green light...

   by what name, Japanese tree,
by what name, Mother?

Dream of My Father's Shiva, Auschwitz, 1942

no water

as far as I
can see to the edge
of the relentless
field

a plow
homes

I hear
the violent
fanning

of a windmill
now

I am at the steer

shoveling
bodies
to find you

when I think
gusts of it
there is something
humming
in the air of this
thick dream

cutting
through the pink smoke
I almost hear
you say it—

this lake of bodies
starts to freeze

I hear
your grunting
when the plow's hand
snags off your fingers—

Smokestacks
finally

in another world
it might mean
the city

where you taught me
about buildings

you're blue as Lake Michigan
when I get you in the machine's hand
the plow
turns to the building
with the lone smokestack

against my desire

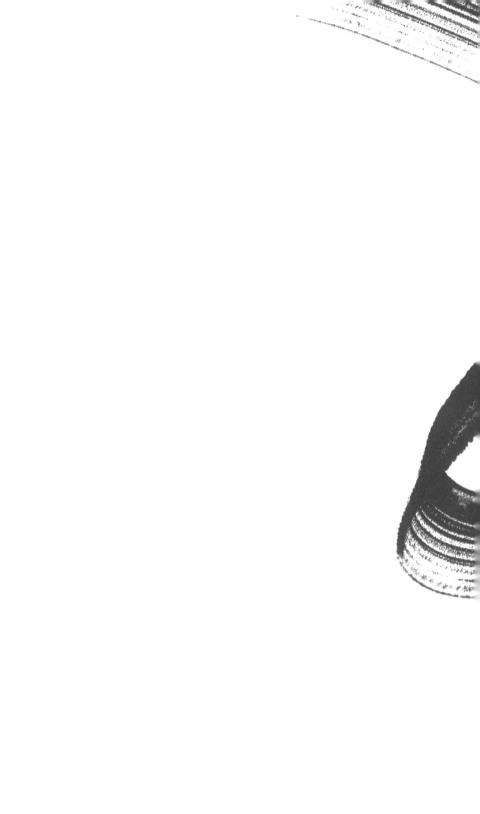

IV.

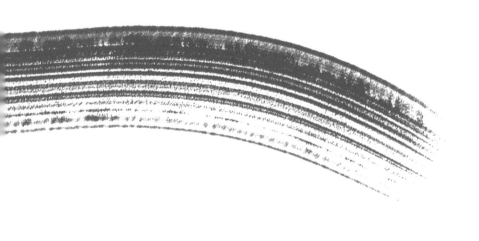

Dream of My Father's Shiva, Atlantis, 1450/3074

There are no orchards. The air is water. Everywhere, curves.
I was meant to serve as a warrior, but here
I observe fluorescence, futurity in the green that is
not green but neon, which is not a color
but rather a glow. Fish I don't know
the name of make Os of their lips.
The only body is the body.

There is an implication in the reticence, in the modesty.
If the city is a drowned still life, there is only one way
to finish the proof: in dreams
we always arrive in the middle and leave in the middle,
as in life, where the only knowledge is
we have been born.

Horseshoe

Lately, I've been walking through arches.
Churches, synagogues, ashrams, no matter. I
find astonishment in the impulse.
The thought of my mother enters me in the monastery
even though I am Jewish
and I know I have not been good,
not heard her voice enough—she is still alive
but won't be always. Though this agony is
always. I do not find her
or anyone else I love in these buildings. But then,
what is it to love someone
if not to love the self,
which I have not, despite my banal fortune.
It was a profoundly depressing thought
this afternoon in Cambridge, with the light holding
over the university, the steeples, the trees—and now
the thought is something else, is knowledge
in the way that it is known all at once
away from the guts,
up in the mindfield: it's a running horse,
beating your timid soul,
knocking all over it with its metal-lined hooves
reminding you you are there.

Inheritance

In Frankfurt, a part of you you've never met
rises through the spine
and locks your jaw:

someone at the airport will know who you are.

You look down at your passport
certain that by some act of the cosmos
the name will read

Aliza Tesviah

but it does not. It says America and Chicago
and Lisa and many
numbers, numbers

on the passport.

The walkways of European airports are endless
and windowless. What if in the maze
you walk through your gate

and find yourself on a train.

I cannot remember what my Nonnie says
about schmaltz, how long to leave the brisket
in the oven, or the prayer for the dead.

All your life's inheritances

in the form of things and lessons,
but no one told you about this, this one
here in your throat

this anxiety:

How can anyone live here now.
How can anyone think this
happened a long time ago

or never at all.

Anniversary

Say the occasion calls for
a trip to the Botanic Gardens

where you take me over
a hill. There are stalls

for horses. Against them
you devised to touch me.

Your mouth is on my
clavicle, the shape of you

-r head in the forefront
of my view of the clearing

behind you. There are
many things on green

but only two things in
motion: bodies, chestnut

like your hairs scratching
at me. You're rough

because you feel my bone
pointing out of my heart.

Skin on the neck wants
not to hold in this love,

this repulsion—nor does
it want to protect from

your mouth, your beard,
your performance. Rug

burn. In the distance,
the mares, wily and sprinting,

could leap clear of the fence
penning them in. I wanted

to be as the mares, surrounded
by their own will in the air.

We came without our daughter
for this: your raised finger

-prints harsh like the edges
of shells. Impossible

to say this without using names:
The mare approaches

the rabid other with
too much love, too much hope,

to save an unsaveable life—
nothing but the sound of violence

in the field. When it is over,
your mouth still hooked to me,

the mare has fallen. The mare
wants to nuzzle the fallen. Look,

there she is, stretching her nose
toward her friend! As if to say

you who have fallen, you who
have no claws. You do not look.

The shape of your head in the
forefront of my view. Say

there is no occasion, no
Botanic Gardens, no diseased

animal. Say we are in the house.
Say children are playing upstairs.

Say the penned in fence is a door.
Say it's the door to a child's room.

Say the child is no longer a child,
but decidedly a girl. Say they are

girls, say they are mares. You can't
hear them rubbing their cheeks

together. You do not look. The shape
of your head in the forefront

of my view, which is mine
alone for a while longer,

what I know about our daughter.
Say you notice the cheeks now

softly touching. Say this without
using any names. Say they are

like the mares
powerless to handle each other.

What's Left to do in the House

The carrots are ready for plucking in the side yard. Pluck them.
The dry cleaning is ready at Waukegan and Deerfield.
It can wait, it will still be there tomorrow.
Write a poem in which a speaker who loves women emerges.
Write a poem in which devotion does not devour you.

Prodigy

A ramp of white marble,
the path that delivers me
from the top of the escarpment.
The grey mottlings disappeared
by the dusty blizzard of sunlight
as I cross the metamorphic
limestone, as my bones knock
along the stone path—they are all
that lasts after organ, liquid, flesh.
I place the divining rod in the notches.
Nothing budges, nothing heats.

I grew up reading while other children played
outside. I hummed
Hebrew with my father
before bedtime, the wicks thick
melting. Who will follow me

down the path of stone?
From the shore, I look up at the grotto.
Lightning, then nothing.
The wind is on my heels, desperate
to tell me something.

I look down at my hands.
The left palm says poet, the right, prophet.
At the bottom of the fault
I clasp my hands around the ruined
balusters of an ancient gate
and everything is struck by lightning.

I am in a clearing on the shore
as the sky opens and the angels come down.
The storm goes on. *Who will follow me down the path*
of stones? And the Aegean responds, climbing
all the way up to the grotto: *No one*

with you on the path of stones. The question
evaporates, like the name I was given
which arranges and rearranges itself

LISA HARRI HITON

THIS LOAN...

In America, the grotto is gone.
There are no grape vines. I don't recognize
the voice of the dead
man I am named for who I never meet.
When God said the dead wait
at a marble gate until a mortal takes their name
my mother gave her father his ticket. In America,

my bedroom window faces Jerusalem.

I hear a single bird at 3 in the morning.
I dust it all softly in Hebrew:
I was on the path of stone. I arrived at a gate.
The word for poet is the same as the word for prophet
in my mother tongue.
And then I kissed Maretta to wake her.

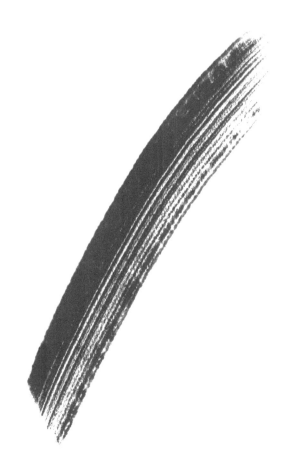

Acknowledgements

I wish to thank the editors of the following publications:

Anti-: "Theory of Universes"
Adroit Journal: "In Response to Trees"
Cosmonauts Avenue: "Mahler's Ninth"
Figure 1: "Inheritance"
Hayden's Ferry Review: "Picnic"
The Journal: "Moon Child"
Leveler: "Dream of My Father's Shiva, Auschwitz, 1942"
Poets on Growth: "Horseshoe"
Prodigal Magazine: "Pastoral"
Redivider Magazine: "Egyptian Daydream"
Slice Magazine: "Beach Fossil Funeral" and "No Sea"
Tupelo Quarterly: "Portrait in a Jewelry Box"
Vinyl Poetry and Prose: "Dream of My Father's Shiva, Atlantis, 1450/3074"
Word Riot: "Dream of My Father's Shiva, Lake Michigan, 1963" and "Dream of My Father's Shiva, McCoy Park, 1976"

236 Magazine, Boston University's journal of alumni work, reprinted "Moon Child," "Terra Vita," and "Tuesday."

Poets on Growth: An Anthology of Poetry and Craft reprinted "In Response to Trees" along with "Horseshoe" and an essay called "That Part of Me."

MICHAEL STONACEK

LISA HITON holds degrees from Boston University and Harvard University. Her work has appeared in *Lambda Literary*, *The Common*, and *Kenyon Review*, and has been honored with the AWP Kurt Brown Prize. She is the author of *Afterfeast* (Tupelo Press) and Variation on Testimony (CutBank). She is the Founder and Co-Producer of Queer Poem-a-Day at the Deerfield Public Library.